The Recession of 2007–2009

A general slowdown in economic activity, a downturn in the business cycle, a reduction in the amount of goods and services produced and sold—these are all

characteristics of a recession. According to the National Bureau of Economic Research (the official arbiter of U.S. recessions), there were 10 recessions between 1948 and 2011. The most recent recession began in December 2007 and ended in June 2009, though many of the statistics that describe the U.S. economy have yet to return to their pre-recession values. In this Spotlight, we present BLS data that compare the recent recession to previous recessions.

Unemployment

One of the most widely recognized indicators of a recession is higher unemployment rates. In December 2007, the national unemployment rate was 5.0 percent, and it had been at or below that rate for the previous 30 months. At the end of the recession, in June 2009, it was 9.5 percent. In the months after the recession, the unemployment rate peaked at 10.0 percent (in October 2009). Before this, the most recent months with unemployment rates over 10.0 percent were September 1982 through June 1983, during which time the unemployment rate peaked at 10.8 percent.

Compared with previous recessions, the higher proportion of long-term unemployed (those unemployed for 27 weeks or longer) in the recent recession and its post-recession period is notable.

NOTE: People are classified as unemployed if they do not have a job, have actively looked for work in the prior 4 weeks, and are currently available for work. The unemployment rate is the number of unemployed persons as a percent of the labor force. (The labor force is the total number of employed and unemployed persons.) The long-term unemployment rate is the number of persons unemployed for 27 weeks or longer as a percent of the labor force. To learn more, see How the Government Measures Unemployment, http://www.bls.gov/cps/cps_htgm.htm.

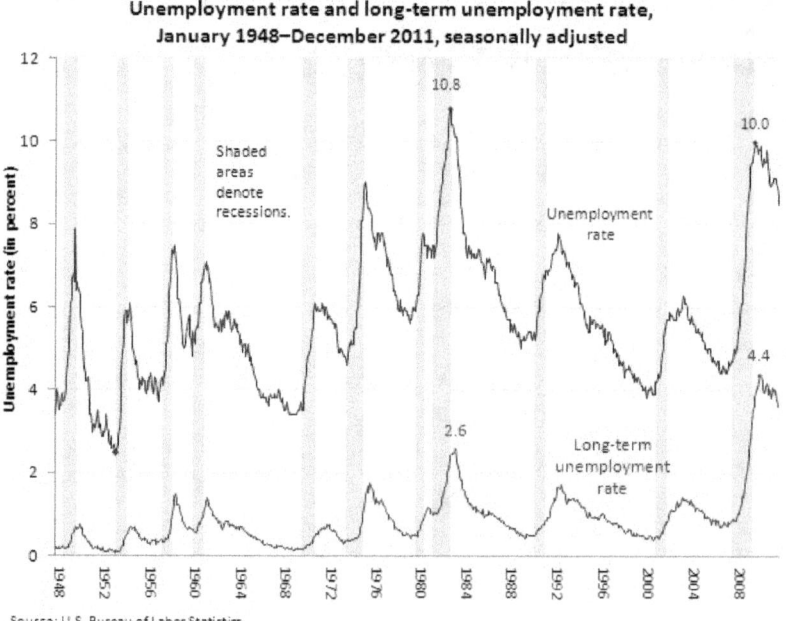

Unemployment rate and long-term unemployment rate, January 1948–December 2011, seasonally adjusted

Source: U.S. Bureau of Labor Statistics

Source: Current Population Survey

Unemployment Demographics

Unemployment rates of Blacks or African Americans and Hispanics or Latinos historically have been higher than the rate for Whites.In the months during and after the recent recession, unemployment rates for Blacks or African Americans and Hispanics or Latinos remained below the peaks they reached in 1982 and 1983, while the unemployment rate of Whites was very comparable to that of 1983.

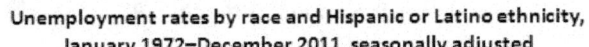

Unemployment rates by race and Hispanic or Latino ethnicity, January 1972–December 2011, seasonally adjusted

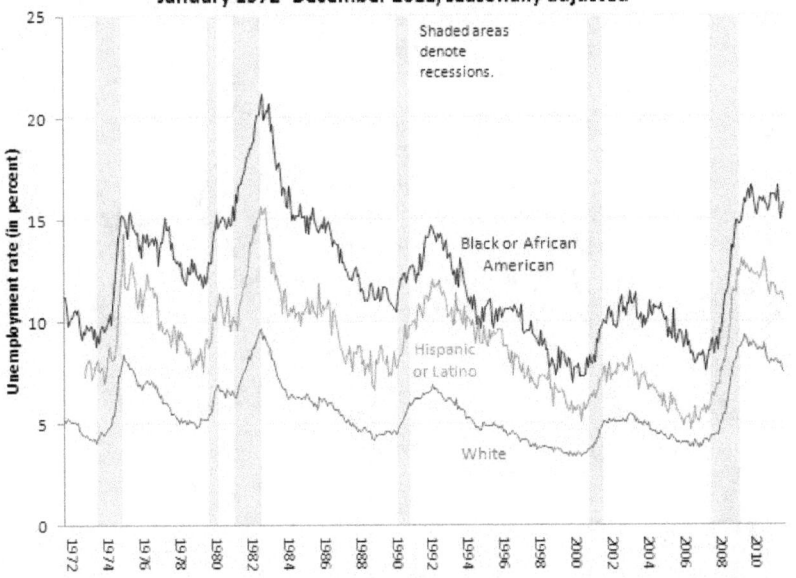

Note: Persons whose ethnicity is identified as Hispanic or Latino may be of any race.   Source: U.S. Bureau of Labor Statistics

Source: Current Population Survey

For many years, men's unemployment rates were generally lower than women's both during and between recessions. However, since the early 1980s, men's unemployment rates have been higher than women's during or immediately after recessions, and the rates for men and women have been quite similar in other periods. Higher unemployment among men was especially notable during and immediately after the recent recession.

Unemployment rates by sex, January 1948–December 2011, seasonally adjusted

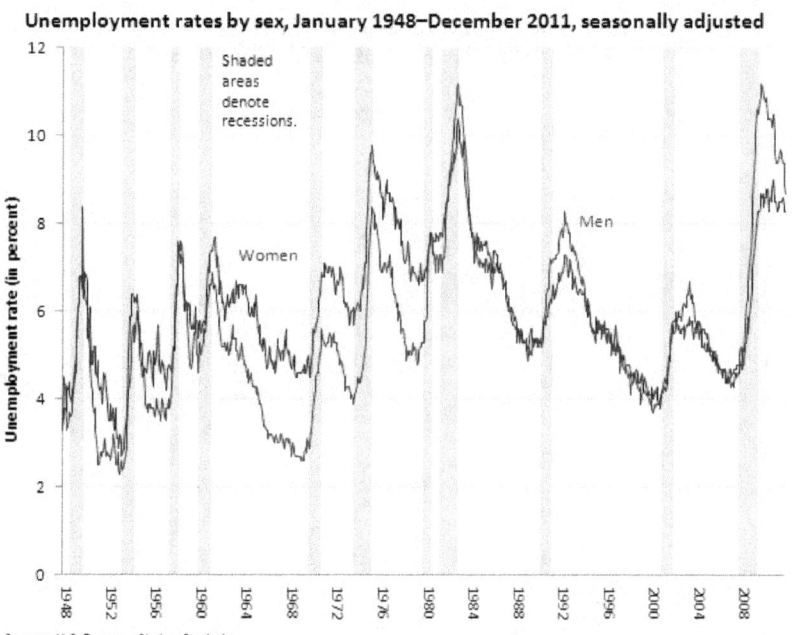

Source: U.S. Bureau of Labor Statistics

Source: Current Population Survey

Unemployment by State

Unemployment rates vary from one place to another. In the months after the end of the recent recession, North Dakota, Nebraska, and South Dakota had the lowest monthly unemployment rates (5.2 percent or lower) among the 50 states. Nevada, California, and Michigan had some of the highest jobless rates (above 10.0 percent).

(This is an interactive chart on the BLS Spotlight HTML page.)

Unemployment rates by state, January 1976-November 2011, seasonally adjusted

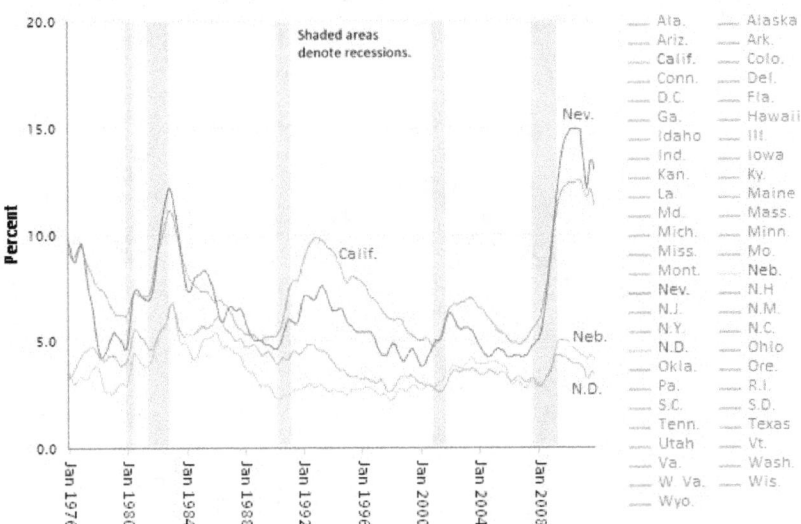

Source: U.S. Bureau of Labor Statistics

Source: Local Area Unemployment Statistics

Unemployment Rates Around the World

Compared with the unemployment rates of other industrialized countries, the U.S. unemployment rate was higher than a few and lower than most other countries before the start of the most recent recession. By the end of the recent recession, the U.S. unemployment rate was higher than most other industrialized countries, and it remained so in the months following the recession.

(This is an interactive chart on the BLS Spotlight HTML page.)

Unemployment rates adjusted to U.S. concepts,
10 countries, January 2007 - November 2011, seasonally adjusted

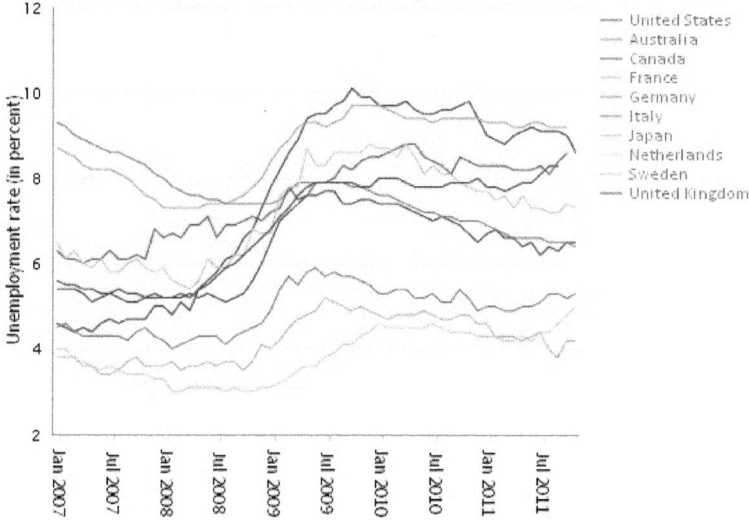

Source: U.S. Bureau of Labor Statistics

Source: International Labor Comparisons

Employment Fell More Rapidly Than During Prior Recessions

The employment decline experienced during the December 2007–June 2009 recession was greater than that of any recession of recent decades. Forty-seven months after the start of the recession that began in November 1973, for example, employment was more than 7 percent higher than it had been when the recession started. In contrast, 47 months after the start of the most recent recession (November 2011), employment was still over 4 percent lower than when the recession began.

NOTE: In this chart, employment levels for recent recessions are set equal to 100 at the start of each recession. The solid boxes on the chart indicate the beginning of recessions. The empty box markers on each line indicate ends of recessions. On the line for the recession that began in January 1980, a second solid box indicates the start of another recession that began in July 1981.

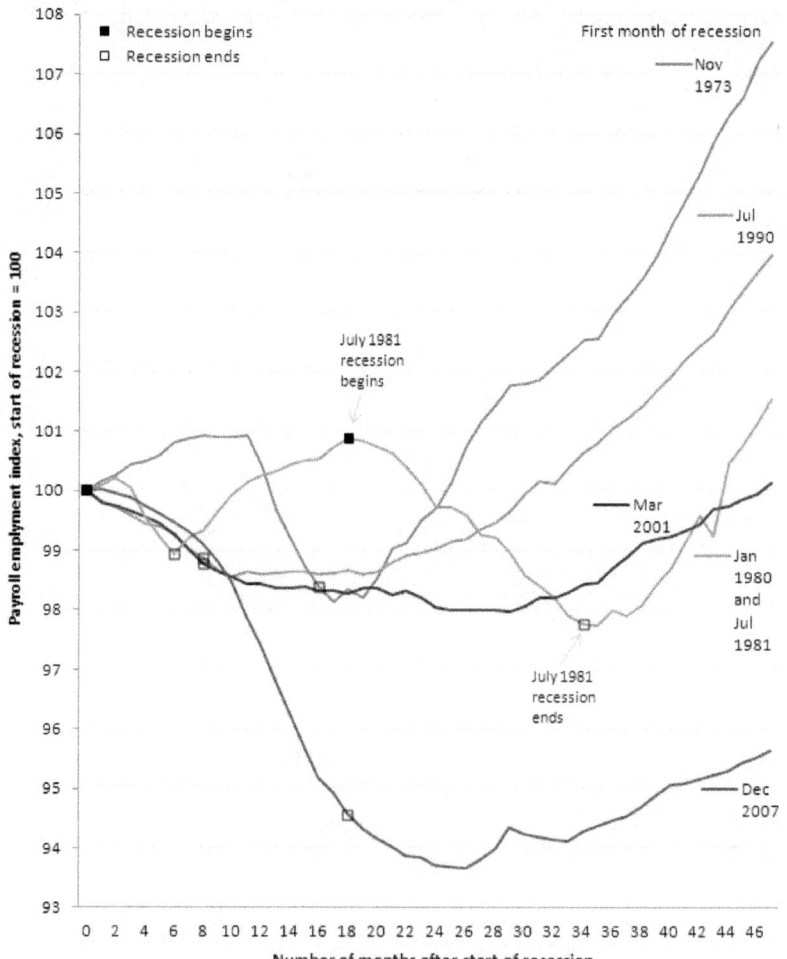

Payroll employment index, 47 months after start of recession, six most recent recessions

Source: Current Employment Statistics

Employment of Young Adults

Employment of young adults declined—as it did in all other groups—during the recent recession. Employment of young men generally increased during much of 2006. After a dip in late 2006, employment of young men trended upward and then remained fairly stable until late fall of 2008, well into the recent recession. After a peak of about 88 percent in fall 2007, young men's employment declined from late fall 2008 until June 2009, when it was just over 82 percent. As a share of population, employment of young women tended to be about 8 to 9 percentage points below that of young men. After reaching a peak of over 79 percent in late 2007, employment of young women remained fairly stable through about December 2008, and then, similar to that of men, it declined until it was about 73 percent in June 2009.

NOTE: Young adults are those who were born in the years 1980 and 1981 and thus were ages 25 to 26 by December of 2006 and were ages 28 to 29 by December 2009.

Percent of young adults employed each week, by sex, January 2006–June 2009

Source: U.S. Bureau of Labor Statistics

Source: National Longitudinal Surveys

Different Effects on Different Industries

Generally, goods-producing industries experience the largest declines in employment during recessions. The 2007–2009 recession was typical in this regard, with construction and manufacturing both experiencing their largest percentage declines in employment of the post-WWII era, 13.7 and 10.0 percent, respectively (percentages expressed in annual rates, as measured from the first month to the last month of the recession).

Few industries attracted as much attention during the recent recession as financial activities, which experienced a 3.9-percent reduction in employment. Before 2007, the only recession since 1939 to see job losses in financial activities was that of 1990–1991.

Employment increased in education and health services during the recent recession. In fact, employment has increased in education and health services for more than 30 years, regardless of the business cycle. Employment in education and health services has decreased in only 1 of the 12 recessions that have occurred since 1945.

NOTE: Because recessions vary in length, the percentage changes shown in the chart are each calculated across a different number of months for each recession and then converted to percentages expressed on an annualized basis.

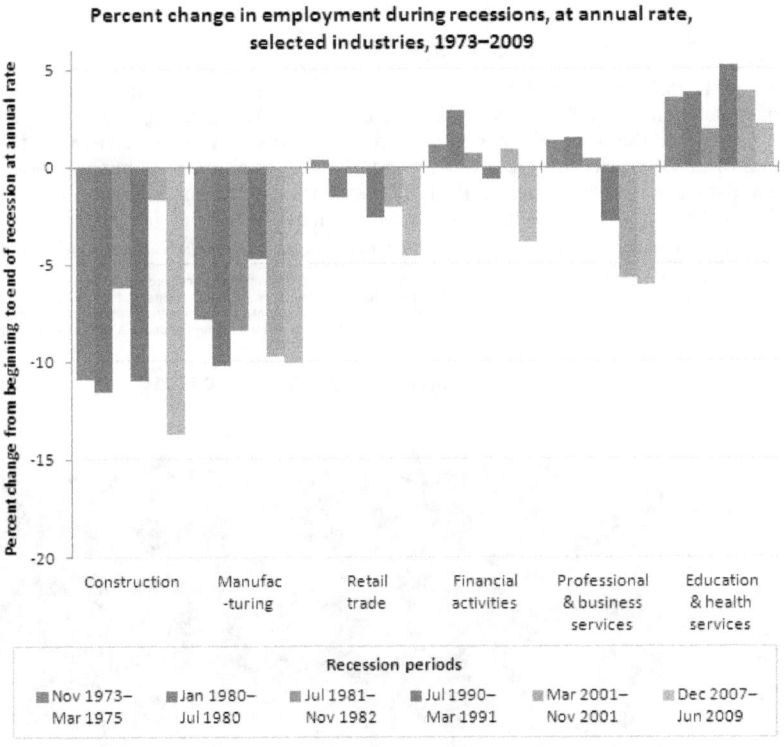

Percent change in employment during recessions, at annual rate, selected industries, 1973–2009

Source: Current Employment Statistics

Establishment Births and Deaths

In lay terms, an "establishment birth" is the opening of a new business; an "establishment death" occurs when a business closes. During the most recent recession, for the 3 months ended in March 2009, the private sector experienced a total of 235,000 establishment deaths and 172,000 establishment births (a low for this data series, which began in 1992)—resulting in a net decrease of 63,000 establishments (the biggest decrease since the data series began).

NOTE: Establishment births are counted when an establishment has zero employment in the third month four quarters in a row and then has employment above zero in the third month of a quarter (excluding seasonal businesses that reappear with positive employment within the last five quarters). Establishment deaths are units with no employment or zero employment reported in the third month of four consecutive quarters following the last quarter with positive employment. Births and deaths are subsets of openings and closings, which excludes seasonal re-openings and shutdowns. The gap between births and deaths data, as shown here, is one measure of net establishment change and differs from the gap between the number of opening establishments and the number of closing establishments.

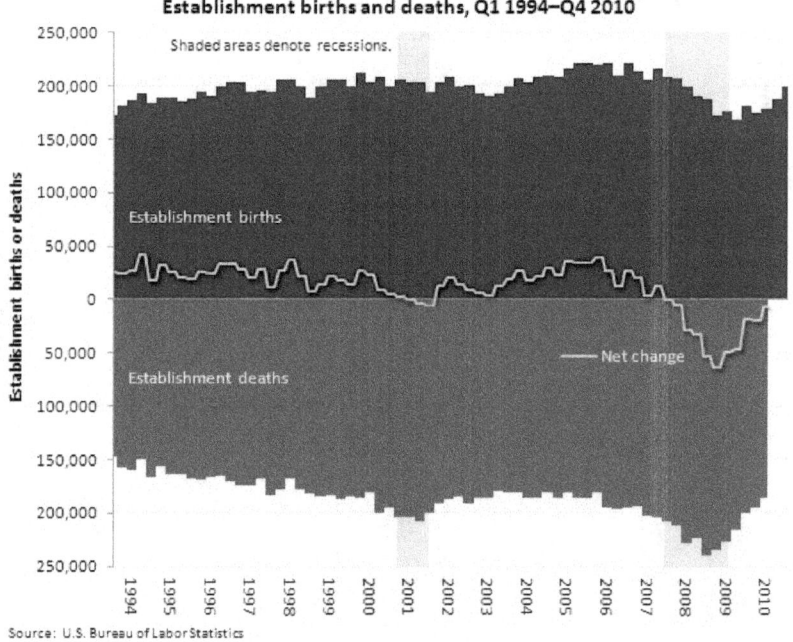

Establishment births and deaths, Q1 1994–Q4 2010

Source: U.S. Bureau of Labor Statistics

Source: Business Employment Dynamics

Job Openings and Employment

The number of job openings, or unfilled jobs, is an important measure of the unmet demand for labor. In the months before the start of the recent recession, the number of job openings, which reached a pre-recession peak of 4.8 million in March 2007, began to decline even while nonfarm employment continued to increase to a peak of 138 million in January 2008 (the month after the start of the recession). During the recession, the number of job openings decreased 44 percent while employment declined 5 percent over that same period.

A month after the official end of the most recent recession, in July 2009, the number of job openings declined to a series low of 2.1 million. Since then, the number of job openings has trended upwards and it has been over 3.0 million each month from May to October 2011. Employment reached its recent low of 129 million in February 2010 and has since increased to 132 million.

Job openings and employment, January 2001–October 2011, seasonally adjusted

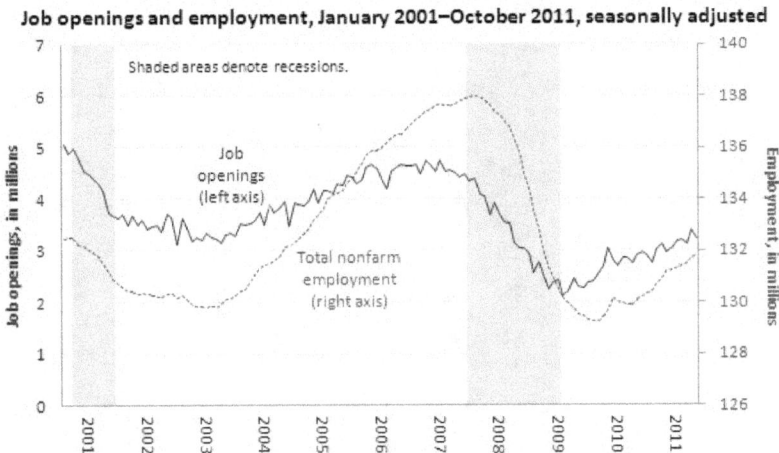

Source: U.S. Bureau of Labor Statistics

Source: Job Openings and Labor Turnover Survey and Current Employment Statistics

Mass Layoffs

A mass layoff occurs when at least 50 initial claims for unemployment insurance are filed against an establishment during a consecutive 5-week period. During the most recent recession, employers took 3,059 mass layoff actions in February 2009 involving 326,392 workers, both of which are highs in their respective data series (which both began in 1995).

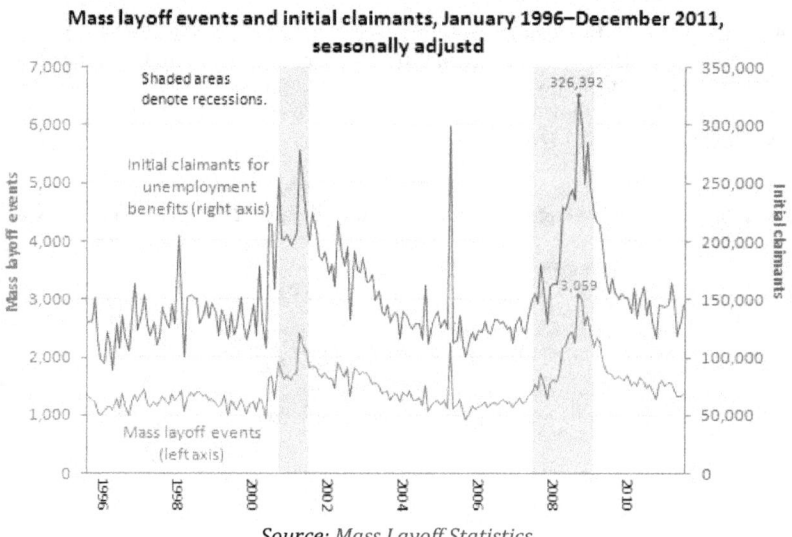

Mass layoff events and initial claimants, January 1996–December 2011, seasonally adjustd

Source: Mass Layoff Statistics

Consumer Spending

In constant 2010 dollars, average expenditures per consumer unit (in ordinary language: "households") were $46,119 in 1984, and they peaked at $52,349 in 2006. Since the recent recession started, average expenditures (in constant 2010 dollars) have dropped from $52,203 in 2007 to $48,109 in 2010. During this period, spending decreased in every major category except healthcare.

NOTE: From 1984 to 2010, average annual expenditures of all consumer units rose from $21,975 to $48,109. Much of this increase was due to the effects of inflation: a dollar in 1984 was worth more than a dollar in 2010. The Consumer Price Index is used to adjust these "nominal dollar" values into "constant dollar" values, such that a dollar in any year is worth the same as a dollar in any other year.

Average annual expenditures of all consumer units, constant 2010 dollars, 1984–2010

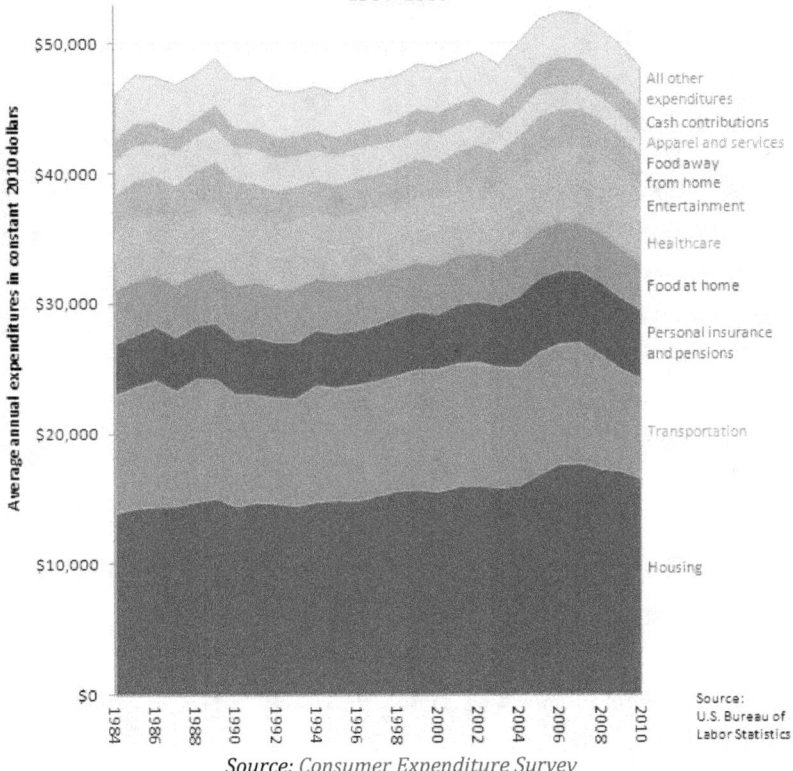

Source: Consumer Expenditure Survey

Productivity

Productivity is more likely to fall during a recession than it is during an economic expansion. In 3 of the last 11 recessions, output fell more than labor input in the nonfarm business sector, leading to a fall in labor productivity. Productivity may also grow in recessions, when labor input falls more than output does. This occurred in 8 of the last 11 recessions, including the most recent recession.

NOTE: Productivity is measured by comparing outputs (the goods and services produced) to inputs (the labor and capital used in production.) Labor productivity is the ratio of the output of goods and services to the labor hours devoted to the production of that output.

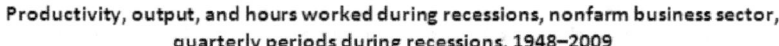

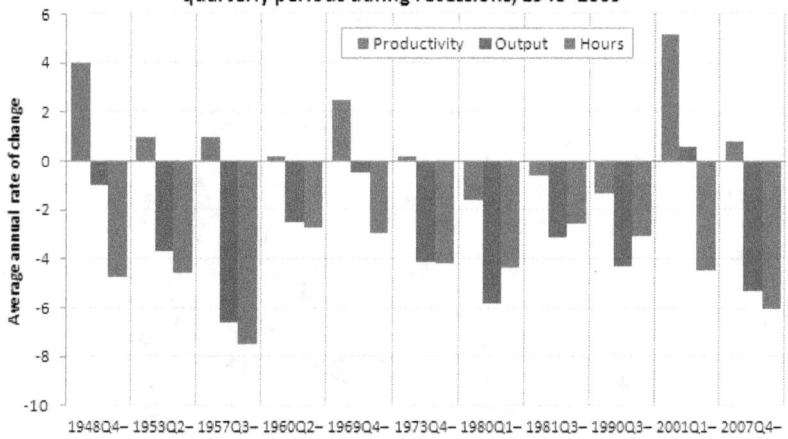

Productivity, output, and hours worked during recessions, nonfarm business sector, quarterly periods during recessions, 1948–2009

Source: Labor Productivity and Costs

Employment Costs

The Employment Cost Index—which measures the change in the cost of labor, free from the influence of employment shifts among occupations and industries—has been called a "lagging indicator." Reductions in the growth of wages and salaries typically begin during recessions and continue well into the post-recession recovery, before the wages and salaries growth rate begins to increase again. During the recession of 2007–2009, the increases in the wages and salaries of private industry employees slowed to 1.3 percent in December 2009. This was far below the 3.6 percent increase in March 2007, after the recovery from the 2001 recession.

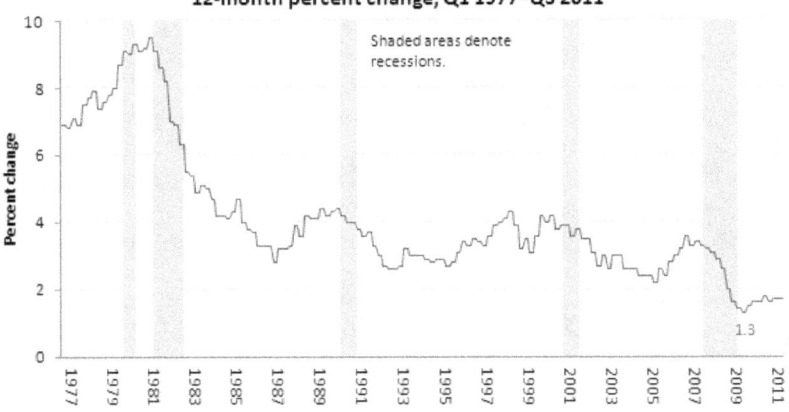

Employment Cost Index, wages and salaries, private industry workers, 12-month percent change, Q1 1977–Q3 2011

Source: U.S. Bureau of Labor Statistics

Source: Employment Cost Trends

The April issue of the *Monthly Labor Review* contains articles on the 2007–2009 recession. Also see the archived articles in the "Recession" index.

Note: Data in text, charts and tables are the latest available at the time of publication. Internet links may lead to more recent data.

General Information

For more information, please call (202) 691-5200.

Media Contact

The news media can contact the BLS Press Officer at (202) 691-5902.

Page Left Blank